ABANDONED SOUTH TEXAS

SHANE AND JESSICA STEEVES

AMERICA THROUGH TIME®
ADDING COLOR TO AMERICAN HISTORY

America Through Time is an imprint of Fonthill Media LLC
www.through-time.com
office@through-time.com

Published by Arcadia Publishing by arrangement with Fonthill Media LLC
For all general information, please contact Arcadia Publishing:
Telephone: 843-853-2070
Fax: 843-853-0044
E-mail: sales@arcadiapublishing.com
For customer service and orders:
Toll-Free 1-888-313-2665

www.arcadiapublishing.com

First published 2020

ISBN 978-1-63499-206-0

Typeset in Trade Gothic 10pt on 15pt
Printed and bound in England

CONTENTS

ABOUT THE AUTHORS

Jessica Manowski met Shane Steeves while she was still in high school, working a telemarketing job. After a few years together, they decided to move to Texas to build a life together. Along the way, they were married and had their only child, a son, who now goes to the majority of these locations with them. It all started when Shane was surfing the internet and came across a picture of the iconic Baker Hotel in Mineral Wells. A few months later, the pair got an opportunity to go with some friends to explore this once-grand hotel. This truly started the couple's obsession for abandoned buildings, photography, and architecture. With their previous backgrounds in photography, this became an adventurous hobby they enjoy together as a family.

INTRODUCTION

For more than a decade now, the two of us have had an increasing fascination with searching out and exploring abandoned buildings. What was once a hobby is now an all-consuming passion for photography, architecture, and history. We each have had our own individual experiences growing up in the Midwest. Whether it was underground tunnels, rickety old farms, or dangerous gold mines, we always found ourselves exploring. Back then, it wasn't deemed "urban exploring" yet and we were just kids being kids (without cell phones).

We moved to Texas, and sometime in 2008 we came across an old roadside attraction that looked like a spaceship. After stopping to get a closer look, we ended up searching for it on the internet. We found a photo of the spaceship on a forum about exploring abandoned buildings. That forum was where we came across a picture of the Baker Hotel in Mineral Wells, Texas. A few weeks later, some friends wanted to go check it out and asked if we wanted to come along. We jumped at the opportunity. All of us ended up getting into the hotel and spent hours exploring it. While we were on the top floor, the police started to drive around the building. On their loudspeaker, they said, "We know you're in there." Then, in a strange twist, they started playing Bob Segar's "Old Time Rock N' Roll" while parked in front of the building. Terrified we were going to jail, we waited for what seemed like hours. After it was clear, we ran back to the car and got out of there as fast as we could. It was an amazing experience that led to a newfound enthusiasm for abandoned and historical buildings.

1

GOVERNMENT AND STATE

Due to the vast amount of land available, almost every type of building imaginable can be found in the state of Texas. This includes many different government and state buildings. Courthouses, prisons, detention centers, and military bases can be found scattered around the South. These buildings can be left abandoned for many different reasons. It may be from the city's decline or because of modern facilities being built to replace them.

This is the Nueces County Courthouse in Corpus Christi. It was originally built in 1914. The style of architecture is often referred to as neoclassical. This building had a number of additions built while in operation. It was closed in 1977 when a new courthouse was built.

An empty hanger on the Cuddihy Naval Airfield. This airfield was constructed in the 1940s by a grant from Franklin D. Roosevelt for WWII. It was originally built as an auxiliary to the main airfield, which was in Beeville north of Corpus.

The crumbling stairs of the old post office in Port Arthur. This building sits vacant in ruins from years of neglect, fires, and natural disasters. Every inch of the property has been damaged.

This is the main upstairs hallway in the post office in Port Arthur. Recently, a local oil company purchased this, as well as a few other properties in the downtown Port Arthur area.

The oil company plans to save the historic building so they can repurpose it into office spaces. Although it appears that an oil company would have endless money to invest into the building, because of the damage it seems like an impossible task.

The old city hall building in Culvert, Texas. At one time, this housed all the municipal departments for the city, including the police and fire departments.

Blueprints inside the courtroom of City Hall in Culvert. These blueprints are for a public housing project by Culvert's Housing Authority. A number of important documents are left strewn about the courtroom as well as the front office.

The basement of City Hall contained a couple of very small jail cells. Barely big enough to hold one person, they resemble rusty cages.

The staircase leading from the first floor up to the assembly room. In our opinion, this was one of the most beautiful parts of the building. The double-sided design and color is unique for a building this size.

An old out-of-tune piano left alone in the assembly hall. This, along with some wheelchairs and Christmas decorations, were all that we found up there. A new City Hall was built down the street and all the offices were moved out.

The former Harris County Juvenile Detention Center was located in the northern part of Houston. After overcrowding became an issue, a new facility was built for the area. All of the inmates were then transferred, and the building was left deserted.

Above: The previous owners of the detention center's property gave us permission to photograph this location before it was demolished. These images were taken about a week before demolition on the main building began. One of the big things we had to worry about while photographing this complex was making sure the doors didn't close behind us. A number of locks were magnetic and still worked even though the building had no power.

Below: The sign at the back of the building reads "Law Enforcement Entrance Only" and was where inmates were brought in for processing.

Above left: The hallway leading from the recreation yards to inside the cell blocks. Hallways were constructed to be narrow for keeping inmates in a single file line while being transferred from one area to another.

Above right: The day room on the second floor. This is where the well-behaved juvenile inmates would get free time to watch TV, make phone calls, or socialize with one another. There are also several different classrooms to further the education of the wayward teens.

Each cell was made to hold one inmate at a time and is about the size of a standard bathroom with a twin-size bed barely fitting in the back of the cell. Overcrowding was one of the reasons this facility was closed.

The detention center also had two gyms. One was on the first floor and the other on the third floor. The gym on the first floor was packed wall to wall with the old furniture that was used. However, this gym on the third floor was completely empty.

Besides the first floor's gym, there was also a few rooms we found that had the same furniture in it. Much of the furniture was large, bulky, and made out of plastic without sharp corners. This was for the safety of the inmates as well as the staff.

2

SUGAR LAND

The Central Unit Prison Farm, also known as the Imperial State Prison Farm, located in Sugar Land, was founded in 1909 and was in operation until 2011. Although this wasn't a maximum-security prison, the history of this farm is full of tragic stories of harsh living conditions for the inmates. This semi-notable correctional facility in South Texas used inmates for forced labor at the local sugar plantation. The inmates were treated as property, and the State made a substantial profit off forced labor.

The most well-known inmate was a blues singer by the name of Led Belly. While incarcerated here, he wrote the song "Midnight Special." The song is about the light coming in from the train as it went by the prison at midnight. The song is well known because it was covered by the band Creedence Clearwater Revival in 1969 and was in heavy rotation on the radio at the time.

Many different parts of the prison were built over the years. This mural on one of the buildings was a commemorative piece celebrating an addition that was built in 1953.

Central Unit was the first modernized facility in the Texas Correctional System. This later addition was used as the entrance into the prison until its closure in 2011.

The official state seal that is painted at the entrance of the state's prison. Quite a few of these have been painted in various areas of the prison. Many had remained in pristine condition for years up until the last couple of years, since people have figured out this location is wide open.

This classroom is a very unpleasant reminder of what an inmate can face in Texas prisons. This room was used to educate inmates and was used as a classroom for the Prison Rape Elimination Act.

The parole office is located on the second floor in the main unit. The office is one of the most photographed areas inside the prison.

The yellow stairs leading from the offices to the different cell blocks in the building. The way the building is designed, there are only a couple of ways that connect the different areas, this being one of them.

Transfer cells where inmates were held waiting to be processed, released, or to speak to parole. This would be both the first and last cells the inmate would see.

Cell block five's guard station. This is where the guards controlled the locks on the doors of the cells in the blocks. The central location of the controls allowed the guards to have a 360-degree view around them.

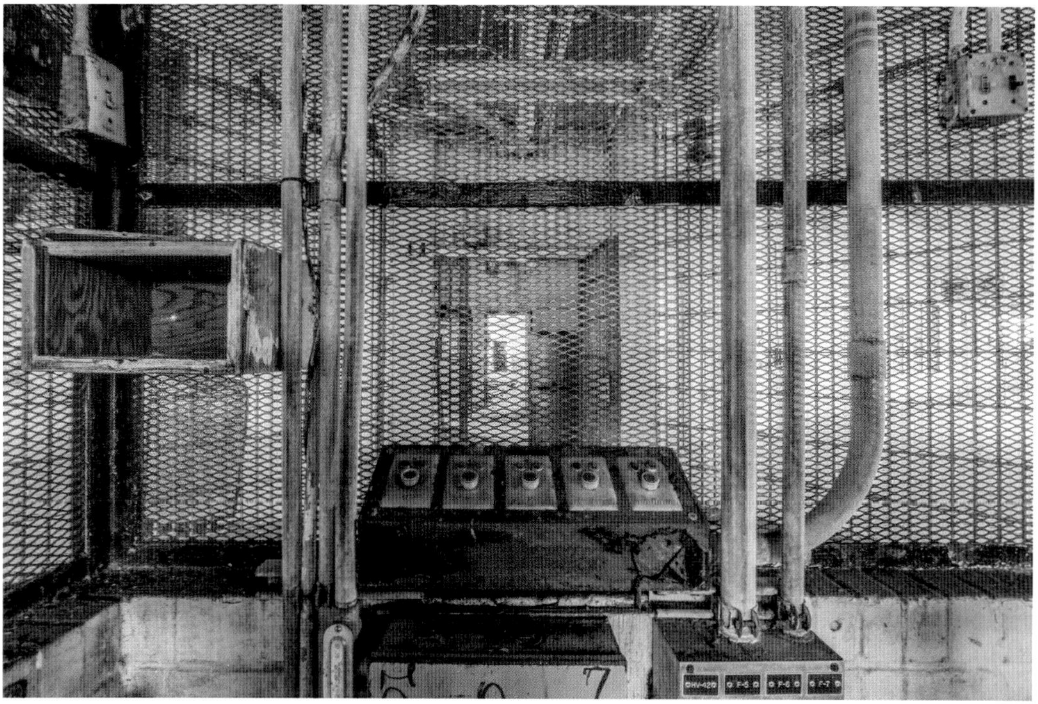

This is where the prison guard could control the door locks while remaining safely behind a cage. The galvanized steel mesh wrapped around it kept the guards safe no matter what was happening outside.

This is one of the cell blocks where the inmates were housed. These used to contain bunk beds lining the walls as well as tables for the inmates to use. This is where the inmate workers would spend all of their time when not working on the farm or the distribution center.

Being a prison, all the levels closely resemble each other with the same basic layout. They were designed this way for the guards' safety, so they could watch over the criminals while maintaining domination over them.

This room is right outside of the showers where the inmates would dry off and get dressed or undressed. Texas is known to have a history of sexual assault in their correctional facilities. The shower was one of the most common places for these assaults to take place.

The back part of the prison was used for the distribution of sugar and other things harvested and made at the prison. In the back of the distribution center resides a pile of state-issued work boots for each inmate. Often, these boots were extremely worn out, mismatched, or ill-fitting, resulting in numerous complaints filed with the state.

This is one of the few guard towers that sits at the back gate near the distribution center of the prison. The fences and razor wire were one of the first things removed from the site. Shortly after that, the rest of the surrounding buildings, with the exception of the distribution center, were demolished. The sad history of the prison remains a hot topic in the news. In addition to the inmates buried in the prison's cemetery, development of the area has uncovered unmarked graves of some of the inmates—a reminder of this bleak part of Texas history.

3

ENTERTAINMENT

Magic Theater

This building has sat vacant since 2008, but was recently purchased by a former employee. Thankfully, this magic theater is currently being restored. It is also being expanded with a new covered patio area. All of the murals have been cleaned up and repainted. Many of the artifacts have been put into storage to protect them from vandals. The construction site is guarded around the clock. It was supposed to re-open its doors in November 2018, but sadly the date was pushed back due to the extensive damage. It is unclear when this venue will have its grand reopening.

This is the entrance to the once-abandoned Magic Theater in Houston. This performance venue was opened in the early 80s and hosted well-known magic and comedic acts. The interior of this place had a unique Egyptian design.

It was designed by the same person who worked on the set for the *Raiders of the Lost Ark*. The theater was being built at the same time the movie was being shot and was modeled after the movie's set design. This dungeon leads into the rest of the theater and was located right next to the entrance.

Left: This glass-faced elevator would take you from the dungeon up to the main lobby. As the elevator climbed to the second floor, many different Egyptian decorations could be seen hidden in secret compartments.

Below: Once in the main lobby, the patrons would be greeted by a variety of assorted magic related decorations. This included authentic magic posters of the past and giant murals of famous magicians.

Right: Even the doors leading into the main dining room are decorated with a giant mural advertising one of the great early magicians, Carter the Great.

Below: This bar was in the main lobby where people would gather for a few drinks before dinner. There were a few different activities, such as palm reading and fortune telling, in this area.

The entire place had an Egyptian theme throughout. Some of the rooms even had hand painted hieroglyphics in their murals. This is where some of the Egyptian artifacts could be found, including statues and sarcophagi.

The main stage in the Magic Theater. For decades, this is where the night's main attraction would be seen. Don Rickles, Tiny Tim, and Frank Sinatra all performed here.

The entrance into the seance room. This is where patrons would go and participate in seances with psychic performers. Several different props around the room were rigged to give a supernatural appearance.

4

PARADISE

Paradise Water Park is located in Silsbee, Texas. We scouted this location at night, but were greeted by the local sheriff within minutes of our arrival. Apparently, the water park is watched by the owner, who lives next door in the RV park, as well as the cops. After explaining what we were doing to the sheriff, and also showing him our *Abandoned North Texas* book, he returned to his truck to make a call. He then came back and asked if we could come back during the day when it was safer. We were happy to do so. Exploring the park the next day, we were able to locate the active security cameras throughout the area. After we posted this location on our Facebook page, we received many first-hand stories and pictures that were shared from the people both working and having fun there. We also heard one story of the police not being so friendly when they caught local teenagers using it as a skate park.

The main entrance to the water park where guests would pay for admission. This is also where a couple of security cameras were posted.

The water park received extensive damage from Hurricane Harvey, because of where it was located. Since the entire park was built on a sand, the hurricane flood waters washed away the foundations of the slides and buried most of the furniture under the sand.

These are the main watersides located in the back of the park. Having the foundations washed out from beneath them has made them structurally unsound. Just touching the stairs going up to the slides causes the whole thing to sway. Unfortunately, this kept us from venturing to the top.

Above left: The amount of floodwater that rushed through the park created rivers for the water to drain, causing additional foundation issues.

Above right: Several healthy palm trees still surround the water park while the rest of it buckles and crumbles beneath the surface.

This is the children's area of the water park. This was the least damaged attraction in the entire place. It even looked like it could still be used. It was situated on top of a plateau, which kept it safer from the flood waters.

The former lazy river has turned into an aquatic home for local amphibians and fish. Some of the pools were filled with tadpoles and we saw various small creatures darting by in the water as we walked along the side of it.

Above left: The lazy river now sits coated in a slimy layer of algae. It seems to be host to its own ecosystem, teaming with life.

Above right: The Big Squirt filling station, found in the kiddie section. Again, you can see the extensive damage in the background. When this water park was open, the sand (beach) would have been level with the concrete.

Left: More damage caused by Hurricane Harvey's floods. Most of the chairs and furniture used by the park remain underwater or buried in the sand.

5

HORSE TRACKS

It should come as no surprise that horse racing was a large contributor to the entertainment community in South Texas. Texas was one of the first places that allowed "legal" betting on the races. These races would generally draw large crowds to the venues. Horse racing began its decline in the 2000s, because of the recession.

As we drove up to this horse track, we encountered a local sheriff parked, watching the area. We parked and went to go talk to him. He gave us permission to photograph the area. After we started photographing, we found out the owner was not okay with us being there and aggressively asked us to leave.

Manor Downs hosted live horse racing and also racing in simulcast. This was the oldest pari-mutuel racetrack in the state. Pari-mutuel betting is the most common type of betting in horse racing and originated in France. This is where the bets were placed.

These are the bleachers from Manor Downs. After the horse racing era, this venue was used for large scale events, including Farm Aid 2 and Grateful Dead concerts.

The original horse track was constructed in the mid-twenties. It remained in that location until it was destroyed by a tornado in 1945. A few years later, it was moved to its current location on the land donated by its namesake, G. Rollie White.

The back of the stands were where souvenirs and concessions would be available to purchase, as well as the betting stations.

The current grandstands that reside at G. Rollie Downs. Some portions of it have been repurposed. However, these were replaced in the 50s when the track expanded.

Rows and rows of seats remain in the stands as the harsh sun and rain fades away the color. This is the view the patrons would have from these seats.

At one time, this horse track also hosted rodeos. This was an extremely popular venue, as it was the first "legal" place to bet on horse racing in Texas.

The decline in the popularity of horse racing was the cause for this location to close. It was then remodeled and reopened in 1989, catering to more than 10,000 people during its first event.

The back-horse stables which held the horses, cows, and other livestock. Unfortunately, despite the huge crowds drawn to the track for the reopening, it was closed within a few months with the nearest large city being seventy-five miles away.

The small livestock pens for the petting zoo that held chickens, goats, and other small farm animals.

We were really lucky with this one. As we pulled up, we noticed the current owner getting into his truck in the front of the property. After a short conversation, he allowed his son to give us a tour of the grounds. Since this was an active farm, there were bulls and lots of dogs that may have acted aggressively if the owner hadn't been there to escort us around.

The grandstand of the horse track was built in 1965 under the name Los Valley Downs. It only operated for two years before it was shut down.

The property was sold in the mid-80s. It was then remodeled, renovated, and reopened to the public as Bandara Downs. This is another shot of the grandstands where the races were viewed.

It then went through a $6,000,000 renovation. Bandara Downs has played host to over 300,000 gambling customers. It was also known to host festivals, concerts, and other events.

This is the concession area in the back of the grandstands. The park was open until the mid-90s, when it was forced to close because of decreasing attendance.

This small Wild West town replica was used to entertain the kids while their parents bet on the horses. This was built much later than the rest of the track.

6

INDUSTRIAL

Industry in South Texas is visually prominent. A variety of different industries have taken advantage of the massive amount of space to work with. These include oil and gas, agriculture, steel manufacturing, transportation, and utilities. Numerous companies continue to thrive while others diminish and die out. Entire towns are built around factories, refineries, foundries, breweries, and a number of other businesses.

When these businesses close or cease to operate, the towns built around them generally follow suit. Entire regions have felt the effects of their local industries closing. In rural areas, these large industrial complexes are commonly not re-purposed and are simply left behind.

Industrial abandonments can bring completely different kinds of hazards than other locations. Some areas may have chemicals and other residue that are dangerous to kick up and breathe in while walking around. Extra precautions, such as respirators, are needed for protection in these unpredictable areas.

The production line of a casting foundry. Sometimes we find factories that look like the workers left mid-shift, seemingly with no explanation.

Often factories will still have controls for the machinery intact, like this control panel in an abandoned factory in far South Texas. The dirt was stained black and the air reeked of oil.

Inside of the old Ice and Cold Storage Warehouse in San Antonio. Construction started in the 1900s and was completed in 1957. Many renovations have happened over the years. The building now sits abandoned, besides the occasional squatter or tagger.

At one time, the cold storage warehouse was heavily used by the Union Pacific Railroad. It has sat vacant since 1999.

Above: One of the upper floors of the Falstaff Brewery. This giant complex was built in the 1890s as The Galveston Brewing Company. By the time 1891 rolled around, the plant was unoccupied. Over the past few years, the new developer has begun to repurpose the complex into an entertainment plaza and hotel.

Right: A rusty control panel remains inside the brewery. The sea air combined with years of neglect caused the entire building to rot and crumble. One of the buildings has been fixed up and turned into cruise ship parking. This will generate revenue for the repair to the rest of the complex.

Above: One of the inherent dangers of exploring industrial locations are the random holes left from removing the factory equipment. This hole in the century-old Falstaff Brewery leads from the top floor all the way to the bottom. One wrong step could equal disaster or serious injury.

Left: The Galveston Municipal Incinerator was built in 1943 to burn the city's trash. It has been closed since 1955 due to new regulation changes. This site was part salvage yard and part dump. Often, there would be piles of discarded boats in the front of it.

Above: Inside the municipal incinerator in Galveston, sits the giant claw used to grab large amounts of garbage from the trucks and drop them into the incinerator.

Right: The view out a side door of the no-longer standing incinerator. The Galveston Municipal Incinerator was a well-known spot until 2018, when it was demolished by the city. Even though the ground is highly contaminated, the city plans to redevelop the area.

7

FRIEDRICH REFRIGERATION

On one of our trips down South to San Antonio, we decided to stop by the Friedrich Refrigeration Complex. As we drove around the building, we could see multiple workers in different areas of the building. The police were also in the front of the building. We then decided to stop and talk to one of the workers at the entrance. We explained that we were getting content for our book and asked if we could photograph the inside. His response was a very quick and stern NO. He then told us how his boss would not be okay with it. We asked if there was any way to speak to his boss. He said sure, and gave us his phone number to call. We talked to the head developer and told him how we are documenting the historic abandoned buildings around Texas for our upcoming book (this one). After a short conversation he asked if he could see our work, which we were happy to share with him. A few minutes later he gave us the go ahead to photograph the complex.

We met the worker we were originally talking to in the front of the building. He and an officer were having a conversation while escorting us into the building. Apparently, the officer had just caught someone trespassing in a different area of the complex. They gave us a couple of rules to follow, which we were happy to oblige by. We had the opportunity to walk around and photograph for a couple of hours. He even sent us some old photos of when the complex was still producing units.

The exterior view of the Friedrich Refrigeration Complex. Ed Friedrich founded his company in 1883. He originally started out as a furniture and cabinet builder and used materials like horns from longhorn cattle. Eventually, he came up with one of the first refrigeration systems.

Ed prided himself on being an inventor and coming up with innovations for new products.

His first refrigeration systems were primitive by today's standards. However, back then, they were extremely cutting edge and successful for his company.

In 1923, the original plant caught fire and it was relocated to its current location.

Then, in the early 50s, they branched out into room air-conditioning. The first units were relatively simple and used ice as a cooling method.

Sales began to grow for Friedrich in 1952 and have not stopped since. Over half of a century later, Friedrich is one of the most well-known room air-conditioning companies in the industry.

The property continued to expand with the increase of demand. It now spans over five acres with over 530,000 square feet.

In 1981, production was moved to another location and later closed in 1980 due to stiff foreign competition.

After four decades of doing business in San Antonio, they moved their operation to Monterrey, Mexico in 2006. The headquarters also moved in 2010, ending their business in San Antonio.

After many years of sitting vacant and slowly rotting away, developers have purchased The Friedrich Complex with the intent of turning the once-used space into lofts and retail shops.

The new developers face many challenges and issues from years of neglect. There is also the problem of trying to secure the building while keeping trespassers, thieves, and vandals out.

8

LONE STAR BREWERY

After prohibition in 1933, this well-known San Antonio brewery was built. Finally, in 1940, after a few ownership changes, it was named the Lone Star Brewery. Later that year, they started producing Lone Star Beer. Over the years the massive brewery continued to change ownership. By the time the 60s rolled around, the brewery had over 600 employees. During the late 1960s, their sales were at an all-time high, with over one-million barrels sold.

The chain link fence that spans the entire length of the Lone Star complex is riddled with No Trespassing signs.

The brewhouse consists of multiple colossal empty corridors like this one. The only thing that remains is spray paint and rusty metal.

The inside of the brewery is huge. The walls are covered with paint that is peeling off the wall from years of disregard.

In 1956, Lone Star had purchased The Buckhorn Saloon and Museum Collection. The president of the brewery had a special building made and continued adding to the collection.

Above: Museum cases and displays lined the halls of the new buildings for both locals and tourists to enjoy.

Right: The museum's original owner collected animals and oddities. He was known to trade cowboy's beer for antlers and whiskey for rattlesnake tails.

After the brewery bought the collection, it was moved to the newly constructed Lone Star Hall of Horns, adjacent to the brewery. The free tour included beer.

All tours of the brewery would end up in the saloon, where people would receive a cold Lone Star Beer.

Above left: As we explored the factory, we discovered that an empty shell was all that remained of the once-industrial corridor.

Above right: One of the few things still left inside the brewery is this part of the production line. In the late 1970s, the brewery was purchased by the Olympia Brewing Company and later sold to yet another brewing company after that. They closed their doors in 1996. At that point, all production of Lone Star Beer was moved to Longview.

The other half of the production line houses a catwalk that runs from one side to the shipping and receiving area.

Left: All of the upper floors flood during the rainy season. This is mainly because of the neglect to the building over the years.

Below: The upper floors are maze-like with all of the doorways and passages. It is all too easy to get turned around in here. This is not a good place to get lost, as there are multiple homeless camps scattered around.

Various styles of graffiti can be found in all the different rooms. The rain comes through the smashed windows to create reflections.

The upper floors are used as a canvas by the local graffiti artists. Several large murals are scattered throughout the entire building.

The numerous times we have gone here, the graffiti has always been different. The top floor of the brewery seems to be its own art gallery, with a strong representation of Southern Texas artists.

Even the bathrooms have become canvases for the neighborhood artists. They have turned this one into a sign-in sheet for their signatures.

Above: We constantly find animals in these locations. Many times they are in heartbreaking conditions, full of fleas and emaciated, sometimes with infected cuts. We try to rescue the animals we can, but unfortunately cannot save them all. We always have extra food and water to give them. This little girl followed us throughout the top floor of the building. Sadly, she was too skittish and ran every time we tried to grab her. We eventually ran into the squatters who owned her. Please be a responsible pet owner and spay and neuter your animals. It breaks our hearts every time we have to leave one behind.

Right: This large smokestack sits in the back of the property as a towering reminder of what used to be.

9

SCHOOLS

Still to this day, the most common type of abandonment we find in both North and South Texas is schools. Many of these vacant buildings end up being repurposed. People sometimes live in them or turn them into retail stores. Others end up being giant buildings that are used for storage. One thing that we've never understood is how these schools can be full of supplies and furniture that just go to waste when left to the elements. Textbooks, desks, musical instruments, and computers can all be found, and are usually covered in a thick layer of grime.

Above: This dilapidated Catholic School in Jim Hogg County has been left to disintegrate. Unsecured and neglected, much of the school has collapsed.

Right: This is from the basement of the Catholic school in Hebbronville. You can literally see out the roof from the basement. After realizing how weak the structural integrity of the building was, we decided it wouldn't be safe to venture in any further.

Many schools become a dumping ground for piles of discarded objects. This gymnasium in Orange, Texas, was filled with old tires.

This school gave us an uneasy feeling as we explored it. Broken-down cars were scattered around the back of the school. There was even one vehicle that had current registration.

Above: This hallway is from an overly scrapped school that has become an auto salvage yard and continues to be an eyesore for the rest of the neighborhood.

Right: What's left of the Emma H. Wallace High School in Orange, Texas. The main building has mostly fallen in on itself with just some hallways left remaining. A couple of the classrooms were full of old rusty desks. These desks are all that remains of the original school.

More desks in the high school that could have been donated, but instead were left behind and are now far beyond use.

One of the many classrooms in the Emma H. Wallace High School in Orange, Texas. Only a couple rooms still had desks in them. The rest have been stripped and have deteriorated beyond recognition.

The first large school that we were able to explore was this elementary school. It was later used by the Boys and Girls Club in the city of La Marque. This building was demolished years ago.

The Conroe Normal and Industrial College was once a segregated school. Smaller than most elementary schools we have seen, this school was used for training young men in trade skills.

The main corridor of the George Washington Middle School in Marlin, Texas. The school was already completely trashed and vandalized by the time we had photographed it.

The gymnasium of the school in Marlin was also used as a dumping ground, like many of the other schools. A huge pile of branches sits off in a corner.

The Mary Allen Seminary was the first black woman's college in the state of Texas. This school was built in 1886 and remained open until 1972, having closed once in the early 40s. It later became an accredited school for liberal arts.

At one time, the college had over a dozen buildings. Now only the skeleton of one is still standing. The entire back corner of the building has completely collapsed and it's apparent that the rest of the building will follow if nothing is done to save it.

George Washington Carver School

Sometimes exploring in Texas, especially in the South, there are reminders of the unpleasant history of segregation throughout the state. One example is the George Washington Carver School in Edna, Texas. In its earlier days, the school was called the Edna Colored School. Very little information could be found about this campus. In 1949, new editions such as the gymnasium and auditorium were built. It was at this time that the school changed its name to George Washington Carver School. The first known class to graduate was in 1912. The Supreme Court finally put an end to segregation in 1954, but the school wasn't fully integrated until 1967. Despite the school's bleak history, it served its community until 2008, then it was sold. The property was then renamed the George Washington Carver Center of Jackson County. In 2014, a historical marker was placed in front of the campus. It seems like it was used for storage at some point after the school's closure.

Nature is starting to take over the school as it sits uncared for. The walkways are slowly becoming covered with vines and plant overgrowth.

A lot of rooms in the school also looked like they were being used as a storage area or used as a flea market. A few clothing items and knick-knacks were packed in these spaces.

Even though this school has plenty of items remaining, it has been extremely vandalized. The majority of the windows were smashed out and graffiti was everywhere.

The ceiling of this room had completely fallen in. This was one of the few rooms that wasn't packed with random used items.

The auditorium addition was built in the late 40s and had been updated throughout the years.

This is all that is left of Barbara Herin Sachtleben Memorial Library. Water damage has left everything inside unusable and moldy. All that remains is soggy and covered in black mold.

One of the classrooms was packed wall to wall with theater-style church seating. We were unable to find anything about where these came from, as they do not appear to originally be part of the school.

A few of the classrooms here were stacked up high with once-used desks. It appears that every desk in the school was consolidated into these rooms.

These desks were pretty much the only school equipment that looked like it could still be used. It's always sad to see things go to waste in low-income communities. They should be able to utilize them elsewhere.

The courtyard in the middle of the school. A once-popular hangout for the school children withers away, left to the elements.

PRIMARY SCHOOL

One of the more known abandoned schools in South Texas is the Premont Primary School. Unfortunately, not much of the school's history could be found. It was open for more than thirty years. This moldy, asbestos-ridden eyesore is a hot topic in the community.

In the small town of Premont, Texas, sits an eyesore that was once an elementary school, but now sits decayed and abandoned.

The rickety old primary school continues to be an issue for the locals. The cost of demolition exceeds the value of the property. The building cannot be reused, because the asbestos abatement estimate exceeds one million dollars. With no other choice but to let the school sit and rot, the building has been used for storage by the other schools in the area. It is currently packed wall to wall with deteriorating school supplies and furniture.

Above: Room after room contains stacks of moldy books that have turned into unusable piles of mush. From what we could tell, the textbooks were from the 80s and 90s and we found a number of rooms filled with them.

Below: One really unique thing about this school was the large number of musical instruments that were stored here. Although all the instruments we came across were damaged beyond use, they could have been repurposed at one point.

Drums, tubas, xylophones, and tambourines were all discarded and forgotten. It was surprising how many different areas of the school these were found in.

The air quality in these halls was horrible since the building was full of asbestos and mold. Unfortunately, nothing left in this school could ever be salvaged.

Around 2010, the school district in the area failed to reach the state standards on testing or student progress.

The decorative window area in the front of the primary school. Surprisingly, as long as this building has sat in solitude, most of the windows have not been broken. It's one of the few windows that has not been smashed out.

About a block and a half away from the Primary School sits the old high school's theater and auditorium. The auditorium can seat a couple hundred people and seems unusually large for the small town it's located in.

You could tell this was a very ornate theater with beautiful architectural detail around the building. It has been heavily vandalized since it is a popular spot for the local kids to hang out in.

Backstage of the broken-down theater. The controls for the curtains remain on the stage to this day. The controllers are rusted to the point of being inoperable and the stage curtains are ripped to shreds.

In the very back of the theater, was the same style of glass decorative windows as the Primary School. This one had more damage, but for the most part, was still intact.

10

HOUSES

Run-down houses, ranches, and even entire communities have been left to the unforgiving Texas elements. Death, water contamination, and air pollution are just a few reasons why some of these homes must be evacuated. We've always kept exploring houses to a minimum, because it's too personal and risky. House exploration is an easy way to get caught exploring, because people seem to be more concerned with these little houses than the larger abandoned spots.

This dilapidated house is located in Bartlett, Texas. At one time, this would have been a neat little house with unique architecture. For unknown reasons, it now sits and slowly rots.

The old Walnut Ridge Mansion in Gonzales, Texas. Restoration on the home has recently begun. Their plans are to bring back the former glory of the beautiful mansion.

Above: The Fountain of Eddingston Court. This residential complex was built in the late 1920s.

Right: Eddingston Court was built as rental properties to provide homes for the ship captains and businessmen from the booming oil industry in the area. This is the entrance to one of the duplex-style houses.

The court is made up of four, two-story Tudor-style apartment buildings with a one-story house at the end of the block. Most of these homes have been hit by the local taggers since the property has sat uninhabited for over a decade.

These apartments were used for more than half a century until 2008, when a hurricane caused a significant amount of damage. Most of the houses in the complex are completely ruined.

The sketchy staircase from one of the duplexes. In addition to the first hurricane that ruined the property, a couple more hurricanes swept through the area, causing even more problems.

Tundra Village is just south of San Antonio. This complex was constructed for the employees that worked at the local Toyota plant. It had a very post-apocalyptic, surreal feel to it because of the rows and rows of empty houses.

Only two years after the development of this area began, the head developer found himself in court facing fraud charges. He was found guilty of his crime which ultimately caused Tundra Village to go abandoned.

From the front gate, you can see that no roads were ever built in the neighborhood. There was also no electricity, running water, or a sewage system installed, and drainage issues were never addressed. A few of the units were clearly built within a flood plain, while others were built on property lines with no building permits for any of it.

A view out of a window in one of the houses at the back of the area. Some of the units were close to completion at the time of the builder's imprisonment. The owner was caught lying to the banks as well as the investors about the progress of the work.

An ironic piece of graffiti on the outside of a house, is there as a reminder of the builder's wrongdoings.

The front gate at the Stuart Mansion. This house was originally built in 1926. In 1933, Marcos Stuart bought the property as a vacation home.

A beautiful Spanish-style mansion surrounded by palm trees is rumored to be one of the most haunted places in all of South Texas.

Arches leading to the back driveway. This path is unkept and is becoming more overgrown with every passing month. As you can see in the background, the property is located next to a lake.

The living room of the Stuart Mansion. This was a beautiful home during its heyday. Even after decades of being abandoned, it still shows the quality of craftsmanship that went into it.

This place was nicknamed the Pirate Mansion by both ghost hunters and urban explorers. There were several large pirate murals painted in the front rooms of the house.

One of the other pirate murals that can be found in the living room. This mural of a pirate boarding a vessel covers the entire wall.

Once again, we want to reiterate the fact that we do not condone trespassing or breaking the law in any way. We have been able to gain legal access to most properties photographed. There are many dangers and risks associated with what we do. This is definitely not for everyone. Hopefully, one day you can read our book about Chernobyl. Until then, we have an endless amount of locations here in the Lone Star State that still need to be checked off the map. Remember to check out our website at www.decayedandabandonedtexas.com. You can also find us on Facebook at www.facebook.com/decayedandabandonedtexas and on Instagram @fatwax4, @squishesound and @decayedandabandonedtexas.

BIBLIOGRAPHY

"Central Unit." *Wikipedia*, Wikimedia Foundation, 31 July 2019, en.wikipedia.org/wiki/Central_Unit.

"Company History." *Freidrich.com*, www.freidrich.com.

Danner, Patrick. "Tundra Village Still Awaits Improvements." *San Antonio Express-News*, Express-News, 20 Mar. 2012, www.mysanantonio.com/business/article/Tundra-Village-still-awaits-improvements-3418831.php.

Danner, Patrick. "Tundra Village up for Sale." *Express-News*, 10 Apr. 2014, www.expressnews.com/business/local/article/Tundra-Village-up-for-sale-5390428.php.

DiMasi, Heather. "San Antonio History for Sale: The Friedrich Complex." *NOWCastSA*, nowcastsa.com/vuvox/vanessa-zevallos/san-antonio-history-sale-friedrich-complex.

Hlavaty, Craig. "Magic Island Begins to Stir in Houston." *Houston Chronicle*, 16 May 2018, www.chron.com/entertainment/preview/article/Magic-Island-begins-to-stir-12919430.php#photo-15563379.

"Lone Star Brewing Company." *Wikipedia*, Wikimedia Foundation, 27 July 2019, en.wikipedia.org/wiki/Lone_Star_Brewing_Company.